Where Is Puerto Rico?

Where Is Puerto Rico?

by Tracy Vonder Brink

illustrated by Ted Hammond

Penguin Workshop

A los boricuas—TVB

PENGUIN WORKSHOP
An imprint of Penguin Random House LLC
1745 Broadway, New York, NY 10019
penguinrandomhouse.com

Designed and Produced by Dinardo Design, LLC.

Library of Congress Cataloging-in-Publication Data is available.

First published in the United States of America by Penguin Workshop, 2026

Manufactured in the United States of America
CJKW

ISBN 9798217244249 (paperback)
10 9 8 7 6 5 4 3 2 1

ISBN 9798217244256 (library binding)
10 9 8 7 6 5 4 3 2 1

The authorized representative in the EU for product safety and compliance is Penguin Random House Ireland, Morrison Chambers, 32 Nassau Street, Dublin D02 YH68, Ireland, https://eu-contact.penguin.ie.

Contents

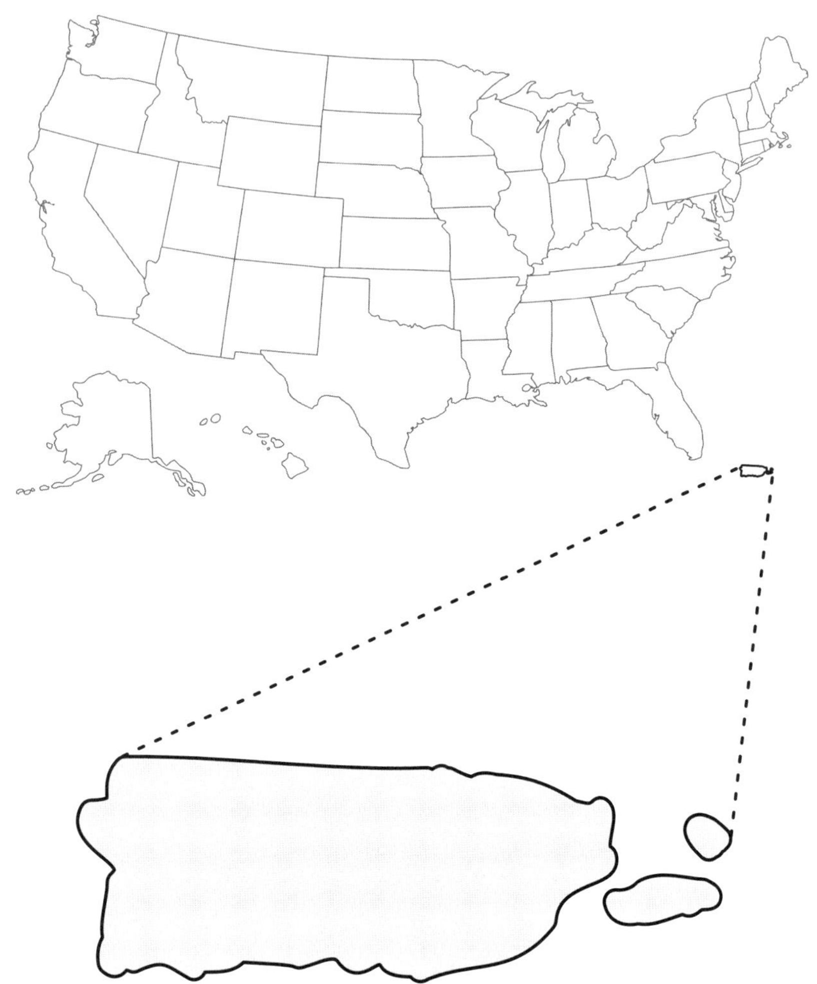

Where Is Puerto Rico?

You slide a kayak into the water with a guide's help. Coqui frogs chirp their name as they call to each other in the trees, "Coh-KEY. Coh-KEY." You climb in the kayak and float into the bay. With each dip of your paddle, the dark water flashes blue. Soon, the water around your kayak sparkles with a soft blue glow. It seems like magic, but it's nature: You're taking a night tour in one of Puerto Rico's bioluminescent (say: buy-oh-loo-muh-NESS-ent) bays!

A bioluminescent bay (also called a bio bay) is a body of water partly surrounded by land that's filled with tiny living things called dinoflagellates (say: dye-noh-FLAJ-uh-layts). *Bioluminescent* means light created naturally by living things—fireflies are bioluminescent.

Some kinds of dinoflagellates flash with blue light when disturbed—like when a kayak paddle stirs the water. It's thought that these small creatures light up to scare away predators, but nobody knows for sure. There are only five famous bio bays in the world, and Puerto Rico has three of them: Laguna Grande, La Parguera,

and Mosquito Bay. The brightest is Mosquito Bay, by the island of Vieques (say: vee-EH-kays). This bay holds up to seven hundred thousand dinoflagellates per gallon of water! Bio bays are an amazing part of Puerto Rico, but they're not the only thing that makes these islands unique.

CHAPTER 1
Welcome to Puerto Rico

Puerto Rico is an archipelago (say: arc-uh-PELL-uh-go) or a group of islands between the Atlantic Ocean and the Caribbean Sea. The Dominican Republic is fifty miles to its west, and the Virgin Islands lie forty miles to its east. The archipelago contains more than one hundred islands of different sizes. The total land area of all its islands put together is more than three thousand square miles. Vieques, Culebra, and Mona are some of the smaller islands. The main island, also called Puerto Rico, is 111 miles from east to west and 39 miles from north to south.

The waters around Puerto Rico are rich with life. Parrotfish, manatees, five kinds of sea turtles, and many more animals live there. Humpback whales come every winter to raise their young. Seas near the islands hold almost two hundred square miles of coral reef systems. The Puerto Rico Trench, the deepest part of the Atlantic Ocean and the Caribbean Sea, lies about seventy-five miles north of the main island. The trench goes down more than five miles and is home to deep-sea creatures such as the dumbo octopus. They're the deepest-living octopuses in the world!

The main island of Puerto Rico is shaped a bit like a rectangle. It has three geographical regions: mountains, karst (an area of limestone), and around three hundred miles of coastline. Most of its people live along the coast, especially in the northeast. Many of the coastal areas have beautiful sandy beaches. Mangroves, a kind of tree that lives along tropical coasts, also grow there. These trees help keep the coast from washing away and provide an important habitat (place to live) for fish and birds.

Mountains and hills cover much of Puerto Rico. The Cordillera (say: korh-dee-YEH-rah) Central is its tallest mountain range. It is higher than three thousand feet in many areas. At 4,390 feet, the Cerro de Punta peak is the highest point on the island. The Luquillo (say: loo-KEE-yo) Mountains are home to El Yunque (say: YOONG-keh) National Forest. This twenty-eight-thousand-acre tropical rainforest has hundreds of animal and plant species. That includes thirteen out of the seventeen known kinds of coqui tree frogs. These frogs don't have webbed feet. Instead, they have toes with sticky pads to help them climb trees. El Yunque is also one of the few places where the endangered Puerto Rican parrot lives.

The karst region covers almost 28 percent of Puerto Rico. It contains limestone, a rock that's soft enough to be dissolved by water. Over time, rain wears it away. Large forests grow in the karst,

and this area also has underground rivers, aquifers (layers of rock that hold water), and huge caves. Dissolving limestone can cause sinkholes to open up—one of the island's karst areas has more than four thousand sinkholes!

Puerto Rico has a tropical climate, so weather doesn't change much with the seasons. The temperature usually stays between 72 degrees Fahrenheit and 88 degrees Fahrenheit. Humidity is high in the northern two-thirds of the island, making the air feel damp and heavy. This part of the island also has the most rain. San Juan (say: sahn HWAHN), on the north coast, averages sixty-one inches of rain every year. The Luquillo Mountains may see more than two hundred inches of rain a year! The Cordillera Mountains block rain clouds from reaching the south, so that area is drier. Puerto Rico is also in the hurricane belt. Nine major hurricanes hit the island between 1851 and 2019.

The first peoples to reach Puerto Rico came by boat from Central and South America between 3000 and 2000 BCE. Little is known about these people, although archaeologists have found some of their burial places. Around 400 BCE, peoples from South America began settling in what is now Puerto Rico. They spoke Arawak languages and were made up of more than one group, but together they're known as the Taíno (say: tah-EE-noh) people.

The Taíno people were skilled farmers who grew yams, beans, and much more. Their craftspeople made pottery, spun cloth, and carved wooden statues. Taíno people traveled the waters in canoes, some of which were big enough to hold thirty people. In fact, the word *canoe* comes from the Arawak word *canaoua*. The areas where they lived may have had more than three thousand people. A *cacique* (say: kah-SEE-keh), or leader, was in charge of each community. Both men and women could be caciques. Between twenty and fifty thousand Taíno people lived on the main island by the late 1400s. They called it Boriquén (say: boh-ree-KEN).

CHAPTER 2
The Early Years

Spanish ships led by Christopher Columbus began exploring the Caribbean islands in 1492. On November 19, 1493, the ships stopped at Boriquén. Columbus claimed the island for Spain and named it San Juan Bautista, even though the Taíno people were already living there. The pope, the leader of the Catholic Church, had decided that people who believed in the Christian religion had the right to claim and use any lands where non-Christians lived. Columbus and many other Europeans used the pope's ruling to take over lands around the world.

In 1508, a Spanish explorer named Juan Ponce de León (say: PAWN-say day lay-ON) asked the king of Spain for permission to travel to the

island in hopes of finding gold. Ponce de León founded Caparra, the first Spanish settlement in what we now call Puerto Rico, on swampy land south of San Juan Bay. He opened gold mines and encouraged Spanish settlers to move to the island. The king made him its first governor in 1509.

At first, Taíno people lived peacefully with the Spanish colony. Some even showed Ponce de León where to find gold. But settlers enslaved Taíno men in Spanish-owned mines and fields. The Spanish government allowed it. Spanish settlers also demanded that the Taíno people give up their language and beliefs. They were forced to learn Spanish and the Catholic religion instead.

In 1511, the Taíno fought back. Agüeybaná II, a cacique known as the brave one, gathered three thousand men and attacked Spanish settlements around the island. His forces destroyed a Spanish town in the south. Ponce de León sent Spanish soldiers into Taíno territory, and the two sides met in battle. The Spanish won. After their victory, they enslaved more Taíno people and destroyed their villages. Some Taíno people continued the fight by moving to neighboring islands and launching attacks from there. They fought the Spanish off and on through the 1520s.

Spanish colonists living in Caparra grew tired of the threat of Indigenous attacks. Thick mangrove trees also cut off the town from the sea. In 1521, the settlers left Caparra and moved across the bay. The city there was called Puerto Rico, Spanish for "rich port." When it became the capital in 1522, it was named San Juan de Puerto Rico. Over time, the city became known as San Juan, and people called the island Puerto Rico.

San Juan Bay was one of the best bays in the Caribbean for landing ships. Other countries wanted it. To protect it, Spain built a fortress called La Fortaleza in San Juan. Then the Spanish added an even bigger one: El Morro. Its six levels faced the Atlantic Ocean and protected the bay's entrance. Later, La Fortaleza was converted into the governor's mansion. The governor of Puerto Rico still lives there today!

Settlers continued to harm the Taíno people.

The Spanish colonists not only enslaved them but also brought European diseases, such as measles and smallpox, that were new to the Caribbean. It's thought that disease killed up to 85 percent of all the Taíno people in the Caribbean, including in Puerto Rico. Even though Taíno people survived and still lived in Puerto Rico, the Spanish stopped counting them. They claimed there were no Taíno people left, even though the Taíno people's language, food, dance, and other parts of their culture were still a big influence on life in Puerto Rico.

Starting in the 1500s, the Spanish brought thousands of enslaved Africans to Puerto Rico as workers. By 1530, more than half of the people living in Puerto Rico were from Africa. Enslaved Africans on the island expressed their sadness and anger in a musical style called bomba. Bomba wasn't only for sad times—it also celebrated weddings and children. In bomba, a beat is kept with drums made from barrels. One person sings a phrase, and a group sings back. Dancers make up steps, and the drummers follow the dancers' rhythms. Bomba became an important part of Puerto Rican culture.

In the mid-1600s, the Spanish king wanted to weaken his enemies while adding more people to the island. He declared that any Black freedom seekers from nearby English, Danish, or Dutch territories could be free if they came to Puerto Rico. (Enslaved African people already living on the island were not freed.) Some freedom seekers from other islands settled in the western and southern parts of Puerto Rico. Others founded a town outside the walls of San Juan, called San Mateo de Cangrejos (say: kahn-GREH-hos). Today, Cangrejos is known as Santurce (say: sahn-TOOR-seh) and is a district within San Juan. It's one of the oldest areas on the island where people continue to live.

In the colony's early years, Spanish settlers and African people married Indigenous people and had children with them. Over time, many people in Puerto Rico had a mix of Indigenous, African, and European heritage. Still, under Spanish rule, people considered white had the most rights.

In April 1797, Great Britain tried to capture Puerto Rico. Three thousand British soldiers landed on the island. Puerto Rico's governor gathered Spanish soldiers, local militia (say: muh-LISH-uh)—or people trained as soldiers but not part of an army—and townspeople to defend San Juan. They fired cannons from the walls of El Morro and fought back. The British gave up. Today, Puerto Ricans remember the 1797 battle as a proud moment. A reenactment of the fight is held every year in the part of the city called Old San Juan.

In 1815, the Spanish king offered free land to European people willing to move to Puerto

Rico if they promised to be loyal to Spain and the Catholic Church. French settlers who'd been living on Haiti and nearby islands came, as well as Italian and Irish people. By the mid-1800s, the island's population had jumped to half a million. The southern city of Ponce grew as the new arrivals built farms and factories. At the end of the 1800s, Ponce was Puerto Rico's leading city.

People who lived on the island began calling themselves Puerto Ricans—instead of Spaniards—as early as the 1700s. Upper-class people of Spanish descent born on the island were known as *criollos* (say: kree-OH-yohs). Families sent some of their criollo sons to be educated in Europe. Some learned about the French and American Revolutions. They brought ideas about freedom home.

Ramón Emeterio Betances (say: beh-TAHN-ses) and Segundo Ruiz Belvis were both born in Puerto Rico to wealthy parents. The men met in

Paris, where Betances was studying to become a doctor and Belvis a lawyer. After graduating, they returned to Mayagüez (say: mah-yah-GWEHZ), their hometown. Betances arrived just as a sickness broke out that killed thousands. He founded the first hospital in Mayagüez and was nicknamed the Doctor of the Poor. Belvis worked as a lawyer and defended the rights of enslaved people.

The two men wanted independence for all Puerto Ricans. They worked to end Spanish rule and for the freedom of enslaved people. In 1867, the government ordered Betances and Belvis arrested, and they fled the country. Betances wrote *The Ten Commandments of Free Men*, which demanded freedom for Puerto Rico and the end of slavery. Betances and Belvis also helped plan an armed rebellion, although Belvis passed away before it happened.

On September 23, 1868, a group of up to six hundred rebels took over the town of Lares

(say: LAH-rehs). The next day, they advanced to another town, but the island's Spanish governor ordered troops to stop them. The poorly armed rebels were no match for the soldiers. The revolt was over. More than four hundred rebels were arrested. Although the uprising failed, it became a symbol of the struggle for independence called the Cry of Lares.

Some rebels involved in the Cry of Lares were forced to leave Puerto Rico. They settled in New York City. In 1895, they designed a flag for what they hoped would be an independent Puerto Rico. Its white star stood for Puerto Rico, and the blue was the sea and the sky. The white stripes stood for peace after independence, and the red stripes were for the blood of fighters. Many years later, it became Puerto Rico's official flag.

The Cry of Lares and other uprisings on the island—including those by enslaved people—forced Spain to make changes. In 1873, a law ended slavery and freed twenty-nine thousand people. Puerto Ricans were given the same rights as Spanish citizens. On November 25, 1897, Spain granted Puerto Rico the right to govern itself. Its first elections were held in March 1898. A month later, the United States declared war on Spain.

CHAPTER 3
Becoming Modern Puerto Rico

As part of the war with Spain, the United States attacked San Juan on May 12, 1898. US Navy ships fired on the city, and Spanish soldiers fired back with El Morro's cannons. When the smoke cleared three hours later, El Morro still stood. The US Navy retreated.

On July 25, twenty-three thousand US soldiers landed on the island's south end. The US general in charge had a statement translated into Spanish. It said the Americans had not come to make war on Puerto Rico but to make life better for its people. Many Puerto Ricans saw the war as a step toward freedom from Spanish rule and welcomed American troops. The US flag was raised over San Juan on October 18. Two months

later, Spain signed a peace treaty that ended the war. It also gave Puerto Rico to the United States.

The US military was completely in charge of Puerto Rico until 1900. Then the US Congress passed an act that gave Puerto Ricans limited self-government. They could vote to elect members to their local House of Representatives, but the US president chose the island's governor and its Supreme Court. The United States also had the power to overturn local laws. Puerto Ricans were not US citizens.

The people of Puerto Rico were disappointed and upset with this act. There were also few jobs at this time, and many people were poor. To express their feelings, Afro-Puerto Rican people in the south developed a musical style called *plena*. The music is based on bomba but played with a round hand drum. Plena songs were—and are—songs of political protest and daily life. A member of one of today's plena groups says the music is like "the newspaper of the people."

Puerto Ricans had reason to protest. Under Spanish rule, Puerto Rico had more than seven hundred sugar plantations. After the United States took over, American sugar companies came to Puerto Rico and tripled the amount of space used to grow sugarcane. Small farmers were often pushed off their land. People took jobs in the fields, but they weren't paid much and worked long hours, sometimes under unsafe conditions. In 1905, twenty thousand workers went on strike to demand more pay and better working conditions. They were given a raise, but not all of their demands were met. Life continued to be difficult for those who worked in the fields.

In 1914, the American governor of Puerto Rico wrote to US officials that Puerto Ricans were unhappy with the government. President Theodore Roosevelt had recommended Puerto Ricans be made US citizens, but it hadn't happened. The United States was about to enter World War I, and the government worried that Germany might try to take over islands in the Caribbean. It wanted to make sure Puerto Ricans would stay loyal and help in the war. In 1917, the US Congress passed an act that made Puerto Ricans US citizens. It also gave them a bill of rights to protect their freedoms. However, the US president still chose the governor and could overturn local laws.

US citizenship meant Puerto Ricans could travel freely into the rest of the country and settle there. Prior to being made citizens, fewer than two thousand Puerto Ricans lived in the United States. More than forty thousand moved there in the 1920s in search of better jobs and more opportunities. Most settled in New York City. This migration continued in the years to come.

In the 1920s, Puerto Rican women also campaigned for the right to vote. They won it in 1929—if they could pass a test showing they could read. (All women were allowed to vote starting in 1935.) Felisa Rincón de Gautier (say: rin-CON day go-tee-AY) was part of an upper-class family and owned a successful clothing store in San Juan. She was the fifth woman on the island to register to vote. Then she went door-to-door encouraging other women to do the same. As she talked with women, she saw people living in poverty and wanted to help.

Rincón de Gautier met Luis Muñoz Marín.

He had been elected to the Puerto Rican Senate. She helped him found a political group called the Popular Democratic Party. Muñoz Marín encouraged Rincón de Gautier to run for mayor of San Juan. In 1946, she was appointed San Juan's first female mayor! She became known as Doña Fela and was elected four more times. Doña Fela spent her career improving health care, education, and housing in San Juan.

Luis Muñoz Marín became the Puerto Rican Senate president. He wanted to bring self-government to the island. Muñoz Marín and his political party worked with the US government to make changes. In 1947, the US Congress passed an act that allowed Puerto Ricans to elect their own governor. Puerto Rico's first elections for governor were held in 1948. Luis Muñoz Marín won.

Muñoz Marín's political group proposed that the US Congress let Puerto Rico write its own constitution. Congress agreed. In 1951, Puerto Ricans chose local representatives to write a constitution. When it was written, the people voted to accept it. In 1952, the US Congress and the president approved the new constitution. Puerto Rico could govern itself and make its own laws. Its people remained US citizens and could send a delegate to the US House of Representatives. However, their delegate could not vote in the House. People who lived in Puerto Rico could not vote for the US president.

Luis Muñoz Marín went on to be elected governor three more times. He led efforts to improve education and supported the arts, including theater and music. He also worked with the US government to encourage American businesses to set up factories on the island. Today, Puerto Rico's airport is named after him.

Puerto Rico wasn't all politics and business. Cuban immigrants brought baseball to the island

in the late 1800s. The sport became popular, and the Puerto Rico Professional League was established in 1941. Baseball is now one of Puerto Rico's favorite sports, and more than three hundred Major League players have come from there, including Hall of Famers such as Roberto Clemente. Baseball players brought fame to Puerto Rico.

The island also became known for a giant radio telescope. Built in 1963, the Arecibo (say: ah-ray-SEE-boh) Observatory was home to the world's largest telescope of its kind for more than fifty years. The telescope helped scientists map the surface of Venus, find ice on Mercury, and much more. It even starred in Hollywood movies such as *GoldenEye* and *Contact*! In 2020, cables that held up a platform over its main dish broke. Arecibo collapsed. It was not rebuilt but became Arecibo C3, a center for science, education, and research.

Roberto Clemente (1934–1972)

Roberto Clemente was born in Carolina, Puerto Rico, in 1934. He started playing baseball before he was old enough to go to school. He'd play all day, not caring if he missed lunch. When he was seventeen, he joined the Puerto Rican Professional Baseball League. The Dodgers made him an offer in 1954. They then sent him to the Montreal Royals in the International League. In 1955, the Pittsburgh Pirates signed Clemente for their team.

Clemente spent the rest of his career with the Pirates. In 1960, he led the Pirates to the World Series and helped them win. He earned four National League batting titles and twelve straight Gold Glove Awards for fielding. In 1971, he again led the Pirates to a win in the World Series and was named the series' Most Valuable Player.

Clemente was not only a great baseball player.

He raised money for a children's hospital and visited the sick. He ran free baseball clinics for kids. Clemente also spoke out against unfair treatment of Latino and Black baseball players.

In 1972, Clemente raised money and gathered supplies for victims of an earthquake in Nicaragua. He wanted to go there himself. As the plane full of supplies took off from Puerto Rico, it crashed in the ocean, killing everyone on board.

Roberto Clemente is remembered as a hero in Puerto Rico and around the world.

One Puerto Rican woman who knows a lot about research is Olga D. González-Sanabria. She began working for NASA in 1979 and has helped answer questions about how to store energy in space. She helped develop the batteries that keep the International Space Station running!

Puerto Ricans also solved problems by continuing to stand up for themselves. Starting in the 1940s, the US Navy used the island of Vieques as a base to test bombs and train soldiers, even though the people who lived on the island didn't want them there. In 1999, a naval bomb accidentally killed an islander. The people of Vieques set up protest camps on the island's east end, where the US Navy said they weren't allowed to go. The Puerto Rican government investigated and issued a report saying the US Navy should leave. The protests continued for two years. Finally, the base closed for good in 2003.

As an archipelago, Puerto Rico has always

been in the path of hurricanes. In 2017, the strongest storm since 1928 hit. Hurricane Maria tore through Puerto Rico with winds of 155 mph. Rivers flooded. Almost all of the main island lost power. Roads, bridges, buildings, and homes were destroyed, and thousands died. The damage was so vast that recovery has been slow. Hurricanes in 2022 and 2024 again left the island without power. Puerto Ricans are repairing roads, bridges, and buildings, but there's still a lot of work to be done.

CHAPTER 4
The Island of Enchantment

Today, more than three million people call Puerto Rico home. San Juan is its capital and largest city. Over three hundred thousand people live there. Ponce, Carolina, and Bayamón are other big cities. Of the islands around Puerto Rico, only Vieques and Culebra are inhabited. Vieques has a population of around eight thousand and Culebra almost two thousand.

More than five million people of Puerto Rican origin make their homes in the United States. Many live in Florida and New York. They're proud of their heritage. Famous entertainers such as Lin-Manuel Miranda, Jennifer Lopez, and Zoe Saldaña were born to Puerto Rican families living in the United States, as was Supreme Court

Justice Sonia Sotomayor.

Puerto Rican people are a mix of their Indigenous, African, and Spanish roots. One scientific study found that 61 percent of Puerto Ricans carry Indigenous DNA. Museums and cultural sites throughout Puerto Rico celebrate this diverse heritage. In San Juan, the Museo de las Americas showcases Indigenous art and history as well as Puerto Rico's African heritage. At the Museo de Arte de Puerto Rico in Santurce, twenty-four galleries hold Puerto Rican art from the 1600s to today.

Visitors who travel the Taíno Route can see Taíno ceremonial centers, caves, and rock carvings called petroglyphs (say: peh-truh-GLIFFS). La Fortaleza and San Juan National Historic Site, which includes El Morro and other forts, are UNESCO World Heritage Sites. UNESCO stands for the United Nations Educational, Scientific, and Cultural Organization. Its goal is to protect important cultural places.

Puerto Rico's roots are also found in its food. Rice with pigeon peas, known as arroz con gandules (say: ah-ROHS con gahn-DOOL-ez), combines African, Spanish, and Indigenous ingredients and flavors to make a tasty meal some call Puerto Rico's national dish. Plantains, a banana-like fruit grown on the island since the

1500s, are seasoned, sliced, and fried to make tostones. Plantains are fried, mashed, and mixed with pork to make mofongo—which is also sometimes named as Puerto Rico's national dish!

Almost every weekend brings a festival or some kind of celebration. In January, the Fiestas de la Calle San Sebastián fills Old San Juan with music, artists selling their work, and a parade

that includes figures with big heads. The Ponce Carnival is a weeklong celebration that starts during the last week of February. It features music and parades with masked characters that date back hundreds of years. On June 23, Puerto Ricans head to the beaches to celebrate Noche de San Juan with picnics and music—then walk backward into the ocean at midnight to bring good luck!

Bomba and plena are often part of these festivals, but they aren't the only music on the island. People also dance to salsa—first created by Puerto Rican and Cuban musicians in New York City. Reggaeton developed in San Juan clubs in the 1990s and mixed reggae, hip-hop, and rap. Puerto Rican rapper Daddy Yankee introduced reggaeton to the world. Today, Bad Bunny is a reggaeton global superstar.

In 2021, Bad Bunny became the co-owner of one of Puerto Rico's professional basketball

Bad Bunny

teams. The island's pro basketball league was founded in 1929 and now has twelve teams. Fans pack arenas to cheer on their favorites. Nearly one million tickets were sold in 2023! Boxing is also a popular sport, and six out of Puerto Rico's twelve Olympic medals have been won in boxing. Of course, people still love baseball. The baseball league was renamed after Puerto Rico's baseball hero and is now called Liga de Béisbol Profesional Roberto Clemente.

Along with food, music, and sports, Puerto Rico is filled with outdoor attractions. There are nineteen state forests and thirty-six nature preserves. Not all are rainforests—Guánica's Dry Forest covers nine thousand acres and is one of the world's largest tropical dry coastal forests. La Cordillera Nature Reserve covers about ten islands. Visitors boat over for the day to snorkel its reefs. Puerto Rico also has around three hundred beaches. Flamenco Beach, on the island of Culebra, is famous for its white sand and turquoise water. Luquillo Beach, also known as Monserrate Beach, has calm waters, perfect for families with kids. It also features an area where visitors can rent water-safe wheelchairs. In 2024, more than six million people visited Puerto Rico.

Puerto Ricans have different hopes for their future. Some want to remain a territory. Others would like the US Congress to make Puerto Rico a state. Some believe Puerto Rico should be its own country. However they feel about politics, Puerto Ricans honor their heritage. Those born there call themselves Boricua (say: boh-REE-kwah). The word comes from Borinquén, the original Taíno name for the island. It often also means their families have lived there for generations. To be Boricua is to be proud of Puerto Rico's history, culture, and community.

Puerto Rico at a Glance

Date Puerto Rico Became a US Territory: 1917

Nickname: *La isla del encanto* (Spanish for "Island of enchantment")

Abbreviation: PR

National Motto: *Joannes est nomen ejus* (Latin for "John is his name")

National Tree: Ceiba

National Animal: Coqui frog

Capital: San Juan

Size: 5,325 square miles

Population: Over 3 million

Famous People from Puerto Rico:

Francisco Lindor (baseball player), Rita Moreno (actress), Ivy Queen (rapper, singer)

National flag

National bird

Puerto Rican spindalis

National flower

Flor de maga

FUN FACT:

Puerto Rico has two official languages—Spanish and English!

Timeline of Puerto Rico

400 BCE	The Taíno people settle on Puerto Rico
1493	Christopher Columbus claims Puerto Rico for Spain
1522	San Juan de Puerto Rico becomes the capital city
1797	Puerto Ricans win a battle against British invaders
1868	Puerto Ricans rebel against Spanish rule in the Cry of Lares
1895	The Puerto Rican flag is created in New York
1917	Puerto Rico is made a US territory
1948	Luis Muñoz Marín becomes Puerto Rico's first elected governor
1963	The Arecibo Observatory is built
1971	Roberto Clemente helps the Pittsburgh Pirates win the World Series and is named the series' Most Valuable Player
2003	The US Navy leaves Vieques after years of protests
2017	Hurricane Maria hits Puerto Rico
2024	More than six million people visit Puerto Rico

Timeline of the World

405 BCE	Sparta defeats Athens and wins the Peloponnesian War
1492	England invades France
1521	Spanish soldiers take over the capital city of the Aztec people in Mexico
1797	The world's first parachute jump happens in France
1868	The world's first traffic lights are installed in London
1895	The Cuban War for Independence against Spanish rule begins
1917	The Russian Revolution begins
1948	Israel declares its independence from England
1963	Soviet astronaut Valentina Tereshkova becomes the first woman in space
1970	The first Earth Day is held
2003	NASA launches the *Spirit* rover to explore Mars
2017	The world's largest dinosaur footprint is discovered in Australia
2024	The Summer Olympics and the Paralympics are hosted in Paris, France

Bibliography

***Books for young readers**

*Buckley, James, Jr. ***Who Was Roberto Clemente?*** New York: Penguin Workshop, 2014.

*Klepeis, Alicia Z. ***Puerto Rico***. Minneapolis: Bellwether Media, 2022.

"Puerto Rico." ***Britannica Kids***. https://kids.britannica.com/kids/article/Puerto-Rico/346196.

"Puerto Rico Pictures and Facts." ***National Geographic Kids***. https://kids.nationalgeographic.com/geography/states/article/puerto-rico.

*Sebra, Richard. ***Puerto Rico***. Minneapolis: Abdo Publishing, 2023.